THE STORY BEHIND

ELECTRICITY

Sean Stewart Price

Heinemann Library
Chicago, Illinois

www.heinemannraintree.com
Visit our website to find out more information about Heinemann-Raintree books.

To order:

☎ Phone 888-454-2279

💻 Visit www.heinemannraintree.com to browse our catalog and order online.

Edited by Louise Galpine, Abby Colich, and Diyan Leake
Designed by Philippa Jenkins and Artistix
Original illustrations © Capstone Global Library, LLC 2009
Illustrated by Kerry Flaherty and KJA Artists
Picture research by Mica Brancic and Elaine Willis
Originated by Modern Age Repro House Ltd
Printed in China by CTPS

13 12 11 10 09
10 9 8 7 6 5 4 3 2 1

Library of Congress Cataloging-in-Publication Data
Price, Sean.
  The story behind electricity / Sean Price.
      p. cm. -- (True stories)
  Includes bibliographical references and index.
  ISBN 978-1-4329-2339-6 (hc)
  1. Electric engineering--Juvenile literature. 2. Electricity--Juvenile literature. I. Title.
  TK148.P748 2008
  621.3--dc22
                    2008043408

Acknowledgments
The author and publisher are grateful to the following for permission to reproduce copyright material: © akg-images p. 5; Alamy p. 9 (Helene Rogers); Corbis pp. 6 (Visuals Unlimited), 14 (© David Michael Zimmerman), 15 (© Bettmann), 16 (© Paul A. Souders), 18 (© Bettmann), 19, 22 (© Lester Lefkowitz), 23 (Visuals Unlimited), 26 (© David Burton/Beateworks); Dorling Kindersley pp. 4 (© Clive Streeter), 10; Getty Images pp. 21 (The Image Bank/Jeffrey Collidge), 25 (© Steve Lewis); photolibrary. com p. 11; Science Photo Library pp. 8, 17, 24, 27; Shutterstock p. iii (© Graham S. Klotz).

Cover photograph of light streamers inside a plasma globe reproduced with permission of Science Photo Library (© Simon Terrey).

Every effort has been made to contact copyright holders of any material reproduced in this book. Any omissions will be rectified in subsequent printings if notice is given to the publisher.

All the Internet addresses (URLs) given in this book were valid at the time of going to press. However, due to the dynamic nature of the Internet, some addresses may have changed, or sites may have changed or ceased to exist since publication. While the author and publisher regret any inconvenience this may cause readers, no responsibility for any such changes can be accepted by either the author or the publisher.

Contents

Some words are shown in bold, **like this**.
You can find out what they mean by
looking in the glossary.

The Magic in Your Hands

 ▲ **Electricity makes amber pick up feathers.**

Electricity often seems like a kind of magic. With the touch of a button, we can turn on lights or play music. Electricity lets us watch television. It also allows us to make phone calls from anywhere in the world.

But electricity does not just run machines. It also lights up the sky during a thunderstorm. It puts the "static cling" in our clothes. Try bending your finger. Electricity sends the signals that make that possible. Some animals, such as sharks, can sense electric signals in animals. That helps them hunt down their prey (the animals they eat).

A powerful first

A Greek scientist named Thales was the first person to study electricity. That was about 2,600 years ago. Thales saw that something strange happened to amber (a yellow gem) when he rubbed it. Small, light objects such as feathers magically moved toward the amber. Thales did not know it, but he was creating electricity.

Electricity was not studied well until about 400 years ago. Since then, electricity has become more and more a part of our lives.

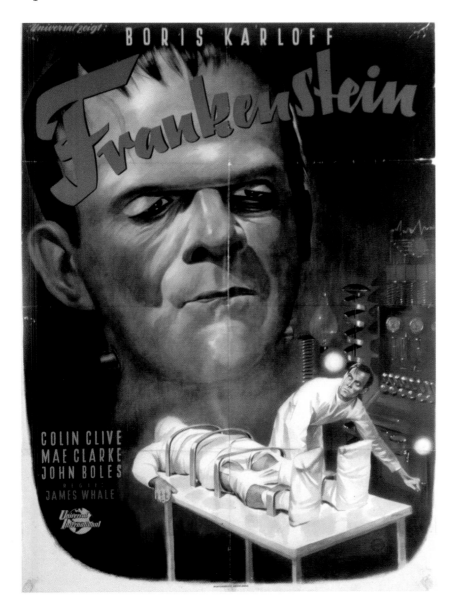

◀ This movie poster shows a scientist switching on electricity to bring Frankenstein's monster to life.

Small Beginnings

▲ Even in this highly enlarged photo of a pin, the atoms are so small you still cannot see them.

So, what is electricity? Electricity is a type of **energy**. Energy is a form of power. That is why scientists prefer to use the term "electrical energy" rather than "electricity." Electrical energy starts at a level so small we cannot see it. It begins as **atoms**.

Everything is made up of atoms. Atoms are tiny. Billions of them can sit on the head of a pin. Inside atoms are even smaller objects called **particles**. Particles can be found in the nucleus, or center, of an atom.

Most particles in an atom have a **charge**—a given amount of electricity. There are different types of particle:

Particle	Type of charge
proton	positive charge
neutron	no charge
electron	negative charge

In most atoms, the number of positive **protons** and negative **electrons** equal out. That means the atom itself is neutral. It has no electric charge.

Power sources

The neutrality of an atom can change. An energy source can move electrons from one atom to another. That power source can be a motor or a **battery**. It could be a storm cloud. It could even be someone who has scuffed his or her shoes on the carpet.

The power source gets electrons moving. This flow of electrons is called a **current** (see diagram). Once there is a current, the atoms are no longer neutral. Atoms with more protons than electrons have a positive charge. Those with more electrons than protons have a negative charge.

How small? ✔

The particles in atoms are so small that they are hard to imagine. The positively charged proton is 40 millionths of a billionth of 1 inch. Yet that is huge compared to the negatively charged electrons. They are at least 1,000 times smaller than that.

▼ **This diagram shows how electrons surround the nucleus of an atom.**

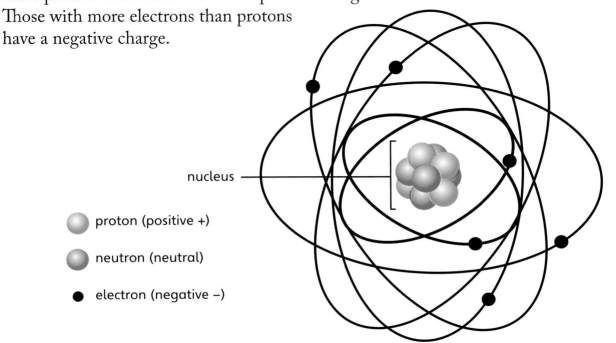

nucleus

proton (positive +)

neutron (neutral)

electron (negative −)

Getting in the Flow of Electricity

▶ A copper coil is a good conductor of electricity.

A **conductor** allows electric **current** to flow easily. Metals, for instance, are great conductors. One reason is that their **electrons** break off easily from their **atoms**. Touching a piece of metal with an electric force sends these "free" electrons zipping around. They make up an electric current. Many other objects make good conductors. These include salt water and even human bodies.

Insulators

An **insulator** is the opposite of a conductor. An insulator keeps electric current from flowing freely. Plastic, glass, and wood are good insulators. The electrons in their atoms are not free to move around. Touch an insulator with an electric force. What happens? The current goes nowhere. Electric wire is often made of copper, which is an excellent conductor. But the copper is usually coated in plastic—an insulator. That way, people can safely pick up the wire and plug it in.

Semiconductors

Some materials can be either an insulator or a conductor. These materials are called **semiconductors**. Silicon, which is found mostly in sand, is a well-known semiconductor. Computers, DVD players, and other devices use electrical signals to create pictures and sounds. Those signals wind their way through tiny parts made of silicon.

Semiconductors ✔ made of semiconductors

The parts of a device made of silicon (a semiconductor) are also called semiconductors. A diode is a simple semiconductor. Diodes allow electric current to flow one way but not the other. An electric current flowing the wrong way could ruin an electrical device such as a flashlight. A diode protects the flashlight in case people put the **batteries** in the wrong way.

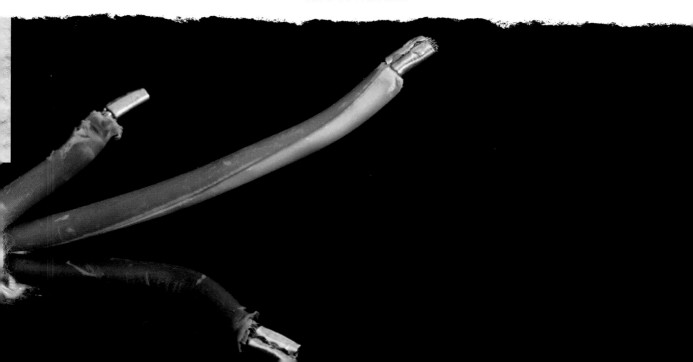

▼ Plastic is a good insulator that makes copper electric wire safe to handle.

▶ Static electricity can make things stick to each other.

Static vs. current

Electrical **energy** comes in two forms. The first is **static electricity**. The second is **current electricity**.

Static electricity

Remember electrons? They are the small, negatively **charged particles** found within atoms. Static electricity is just a buildup or reduction of electrons. Once this negative charge builds up, it attracts objects that have the opposite charge. Rub a balloon on your shirt. This builds up a static electric charge on the balloon. The balloon can stick to your shirt.

The static charge can also be released. Scuff your shoes on the carpet. This builds up a static electric charge on you. Then touch a doorknob. The shock you receive is a static electric charge. It is being released from you to the doorknob.

Current electricity

Current electricity is a constant current, or flow, of electrons. The electrons move from one object to another. They move through a conductor. For instance, electrons flow out of a wall plug through a metal wire and into your refrigerator and back. The electrical energy keeps your food cool.

▼ Electric current can affect the way a compass needle behaves.

Electromagnetism

Earth creates a weak magnetic field (an area with magnetic pull). That causes all compass needles to point north or south. But in 1820 the Danish scientist Hans Christian Oersted noticed a compass acting strangely. The needle wiggled wildly when near an electric current. Building upon this, that same year the French scientist André-Marie Ampère showed the relationship between magnetism and electrical energy. Today, scientists call this relationship **electromagnetism**. Electromagnetism is also magnetism that can be created by an electric current (see page 20).

Circuits

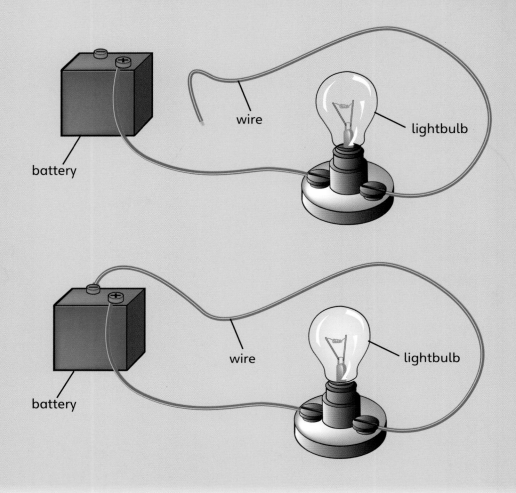

battery — wire — lightbulb

battery — wire — lightbulb

▲ All the parts of a circuit need to be joined together for the electricity to flow through it.

A **circuit** is a circular path that electricity travels along. You can use wires to hook up a lightbulb to a **battery** (see the diagram above). This closes, or completes, the circuit. The negative side of the battery pushes away negatively **charged electrons**. On the positive side, the battery pulls in negatively charged electrons. This causes electrons to race through the battery and the bulb in a circular flow. As a result, the light turns on.

One big circuit

Flipping on a light switch at home closes a circuit as well. This circuit goes all the way back to a **power station**. This is a building that generates electricity (see the diagram below). The process follows these steps:

1. Most power stations make heat **energy** by burning a fuel, such as coal, natural gas, or oil. Some plants use nuclear power. This is power created by splitting **atoms**. A few use wind or solar power (see page 27).

2. Burning the fuel creates steam. The steam turns a machine called a **generator**. A generator creates electrical energy.

3. The generator pushes and pulls electrons along a wire.

4. Wires called transmission lines carry the electrical energy long distances.

5. These lead to power lines in your neighborhood.

6. The power lines lead to your house.

7. Flipping the switch completes the circuit. A light turns on.

▼ **This diagram shows how the electricity we use at home flows along a circuit.**

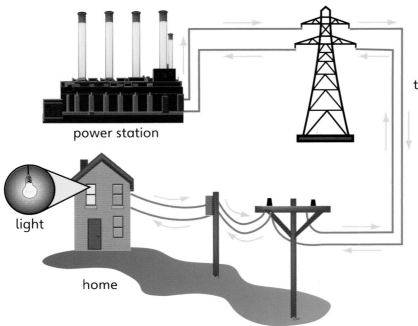

power station

transmission lines

light

home

On a circuit, an electric current follows a planned path. Usually it moves down wires. A **short circuit** happens when the electric current takes an unplanned shortcut. It often happens when the metal parts of two wires touch. Both wires quickly become overloaded with electrical current. The wires get very hot and can cause a fire.

AC/DC

Electric current can be delivered in one of two ways. At first, the most common was **direct current (DC)**. The flow of electrical charges goes only one way in a DC circuit. It moves like runners racing around a track. The current is steady and does not stop until the circuit is broken. Just about anything powered by a battery uses DC—flashlights, radios, and more. Cars also use DC to light up headlights and dashboard lights.

People found that DC did not travel well over long distances. So, they began using **alternating current (AC)**. AC charges vibrate back and forth very quickly along long-distance wires. It is like watching two tennis players batting a ball back and forth. But the ball is moving at the speed of light. AC is used to send electrical energy through power lines. That electrical energy goes to homes and businesses.

▶ A toaster uses alternating electric current.

Nikola Tesla

In 1883 U.S. scientist Nikola Tesla invented the first AC motor. AC worked better than DC for sending electricity long distances. Tesla invented many other things. For instance, he invented fluorescent lights. Tesla also did a lot of work on radio. His inventions helped make radio possible.

▲ As a result of Tesla's many experiments, electricity has become something we use every day.

A Short History of Electricity

A series of scientists helped discover all we know about electrical energy today.

Studying static

In 1660 a German inventor named Otto von Guericke invented a machine that produced **static electricity**. Later scientists used this to study electricity.

In the mid-1700s the U.S. inventor and politician Benjamin Franklin set out to learn more about electricity. Franklin did many experiments. They showed him that static electricity looked a lot like lightning. But it was smaller. Franklin realized that lightning was a type of electrical energy.

This was a huge discovery. At the time, lightning was a big problem. Lightning often hit tall buildings, such as church steeples. This caused deadly fires. People rang church bells to warn others of bad weather. Lightning sometimes struck and killed the bell ringers.

◀ **This portrait of Benjamin Franklin shows his interest in the study of electricity.**

1660
German inventor Otto von Guericke invents a machine that produces static electricity.

1650   1700

The lightning rod

Franklin invented the **lightning rod**. A lightning rod is a metal pole with a wire attached. Franklin put his lightning rod on tall buildings. Then he ran the wire down to the ground. Lightning tends to hit the rod. This is because it is the highest object on the roof. The electricity followed the wire. It went harmlessly to the ground. Franklin's invention is still used on tall buildings today.

The battery

In 1800 an Italian scientist named Alessandro Volta created the first **battery**. A battery is something that uses metal and chemicals to create electrical energy (see page 21). Batteries would one day become essential power sources for modern electricity.

▲ This photo shows a streak of lightning striking a lightning rod on top of a building in Sydney, Australia.

The volt

Many electrical terms are named after their inventors. A volt (named after Alessandro Volta) measures the force driving electricity along a **current**.

1752
U.S. inventor and politician Benjamin Franklin shows that lightning is a buildup of static electricity.

1800
Italian scientist Alessandro Volta creates the first battery.

Michael Faraday

In 1821 the English scientist Michael Faraday invented an early form of the electric motor (see pages 20–21). This was the first time a magnet and electric current were used to create mechanical motion (motion involving machines). Faraday later discovered a dynamo. It did just the opposite. It converted mechanical motion into electrical energy. This new power source would lead to the electrical **generators** we rely on today.

Thomas Edison and the next step

In 1879 the U.S. inventor Thomas Edison created the first working lightbulb. At the time, many people used candles for light. Others used kerosene (a kind of oil) and gas lamps. All of these were smelly and caused fires. Edison's lightbulb had the potential to change all this.

The telegraph

By the mid-1800s there were new machines that ran on electrical energy. One of the most important was the telegraph. It sent messages down a wire using electric **charges**.

▶ Thomas Edison is shown here with a replica of the first working lightbulb.

1821
English scientist Michael Faraday invents an early version of the electric motor.

1831
Faraday discovers the dynamo. It converts mechanical motion into electrical energy.

1837
U.S. inventor Samuel Morse invents the telegraph.

1820   1830   1840   1850

People had no way to get electricity into their homes. So, Edison began building an electric **power station**. On September 4, 1882, Edison flipped a switch at the Pearl Street Power Station in New York City. This lit up the homes and businesses of 85 customers. They were the first people to enjoy electric lighting.

▲ Edison also invented this voice-recording machine. He called it a graphaphone.

Power to thousands

In 1883 the U.S. scientist Nikola Tesla found a way to make electrical energy travel longer distances. He did so by using **alternating current (AC)** power (see pages 14–15). Power stations could now supply power for hundreds of miles and to thousands of people. The demand for electricity caught on. Today, most people cannot imagine life without electricity.

1879	**1882**	**1883**
U.S. inventor Thomas Edison invents the first working lightbulb.	Edison's Pearl Street Power Station brings electricity into homes and businesses.	U.S. scientist Nikola Tesla invents a motor that creates alternating current.

An Electric World

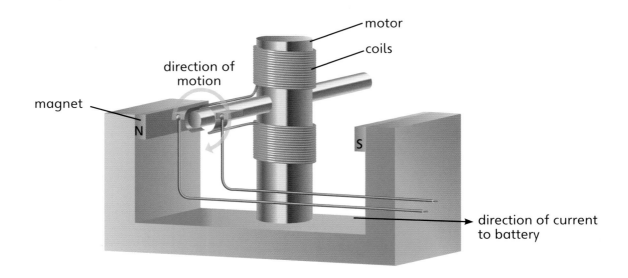

motor

coils

direction of
motion

magnet

N

S

direction of current
to battery

▲ **Electric motors use electromagnets and magnets to create a turning motion.**

The inventions of the 1800s and 1900s led to power sources for everything from toys to space shuttles. Here's how some of them work.

Electric motors and electromagnets

To understand the electric motor, you first need to understand **electromagnets**. These are magnets created by using electric **current**.

You can create your own electromagnet by wrapping wire 10 times around a large nail. Hook the wire up to both ends of a **battery**. Electricity flows through the wire. This causes the nail to act like a magnet. Remember that opposites attract in both magnetism and electricity. Take a bar magnet and move the positive end close to the nail electromagnet. The bar magnet will be pulled toward the negative side of the electromagnet. It will be pushed away from the positive side.

Electric motor

An electric motor's job is to turn electricity into motion. Each motor has a loop of wire called a coil (see diagram). This coil is hung between two bar magnets. Electric current flows through the coil. That turns the coil into an electromagnet. The coil is pulled toward one of the magnets. But it is pushed away from the other. This causes the coil to spin. The spinning coil powers the machine.

How batteries work

Many modern machines get their electrical **energy** from batteries. Batteries work thanks to a change in chemicals. The change takes place between two metals called electrodes. A fluid called an electrolyte triggers the change between the metals. Batteries can be made using many different metals and chemicals.

▼ Batteries can be made of many everyday things. Potatoes are being used here to run an electric clock.

The Body Electric

▲ Machines can detect the electricity in the human body.

Electric **charges** hold our bodies together. The charges within each **atom** of a body are attracted to charges in other atoms. Without that attraction, our bodies and everything else in the universe would fly apart into billions of tiny pieces.

Electrical **energy** also makes our organs work. Nerves carry electrical signals throughout our bodies. For instance, a group of nerves within the heart sends out electric signals that make it pump. These signals are weak. It takes a machine called an electrocardiogram (ECG) to detect them. The ECG shows the heart's electrical signals as a series of wavy lines.

The brain sends electric signals throughout the body. These signals tell muscles to move and make organs work. A machine called the electroencephalograph (EEG) shows electric signals in the brain.

Shocking creatures

Animal bodies work thanks to electricity as well. Some animals can go a step further. They produce electricity—a lot of it. Electric eels use electrical energy to stun their prey (the animals they eat). Touching an electric eel does not kill people. But it would give them a terrible shock. Most people would feel pain for hours afterward. Such a shock can kill or disable smaller animals.

The ants go marching

In 2002 people in Houston, Texas, noticed ants crawling in and out of their computers. Ants took over other electrical devices as well. These unusual ants accidentally came to Texas from overseas on a ship. Nobody knows why they like electric objects so much. But they can do a great deal of damage. Often they chew through the coatings that protect electrical wires. This causes **short circuits** that can destroy the machines.

▼ The electric eel uses the electricity in its own body to stun smaller animals to eat.

Saving Energy

▲ Lightbulbs like this one use less energy than other types of lightbulb.

Electricity is a clean type of **energy**. The **electrons** traveling through wires at home do not **pollute** (dirty the air). Unfortunately, making electricity does pollute. People have to burn fuels such as coal and oil to make electrical energy. Burning these fuels causes pollution.

If people cut the amount of electricity they use, they cut pollution. Many types of fuel, such as oil and coal, are in high demand around the world. This makes them expensive. People can also save money on these items if they cut back their energy use.

Energy-saving tips

To save energy, try some of these tips at home:

- Roughly half of all energy use at home goes to heating and cooling. Use less air conditioning and heat.

- About one-third of energy goes to lights, stoves, and other machines. Turn off these machines when they are not in use.

- Buy appliances that use less energy. Also, use fluorescent lightbulbs instead of the old-fashioned incandescent lightbulbs. They use less energy.

▼ **Electricity travels across the country along power lines.**

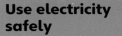

An Electric Future

▲ Solar panels can be used to charge cell phones.

Electrical **energy** has changed the world in many ways. But not all of them have been good.

Fuels such as oil and coal are burned to create electrical energy. Those fuels do not just **pollute** the air and water. They have also changed Earth's climate (weather patterns). Earth's temperature is rising at a rate of 1.1 to 2.2 degrees Celsius (2 to 4 degrees Fahrenheit) every 100 years. That is enough to melt ice at the North and South poles. With that comes rising seas. Rising temperatures also cause unusually strong storms worldwide.

Using the sun and wind

We need new, "cleaner" ways to produce electrical energy. One of the biggest ways is to use solar panels. They are made mostly of silicon and glass. Solar panels capture the energy from the sun and turn it into electricity. They are expensive to install but more and more homes and businesses are using them.

Another energy source is wind. Wind spins giant wind mills. This creates power that can be turned into electrical energy. But the wind does not blow all the time. So, people cannot always rely on wind power. Also, few power lines have been built to places that are windy. That means the power cannot be sent to people's homes.

The ways to produce electrical energy may change over time. But electrical energy will always remain an important part of our lives.

Electric cars

Oil supplies will run out one day. So, many people are turning to electric cars. Some cars get their power by being plugged into an electric socket. Others are called hybrids. Their engines use gasoline part of the time. Other times they run off an electric **battery**.

▼ **This electric car is having its battery charged.**

Timeline

(These dates are often approximations.)

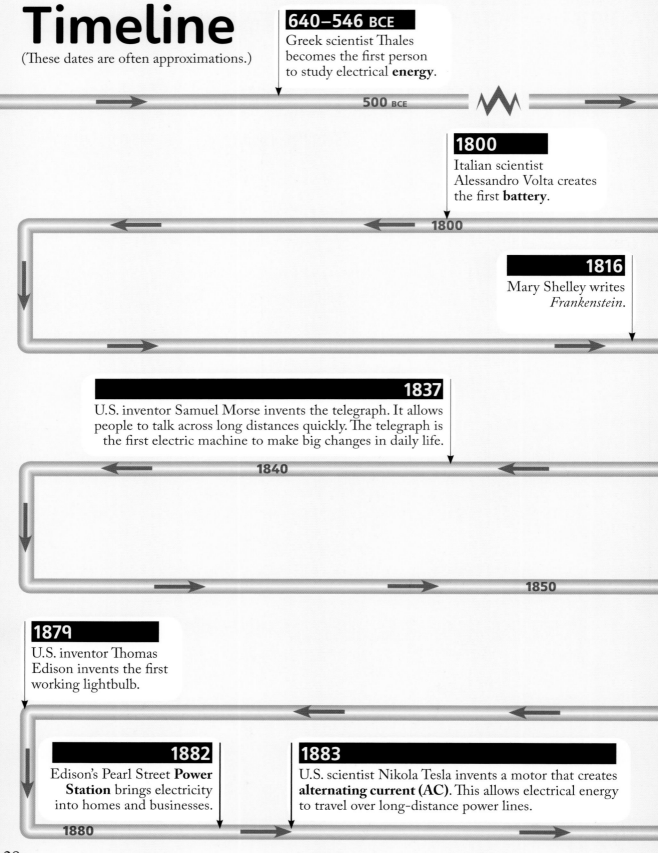

640–546 BCE
Greek scientist Thales becomes the first person to study electrical **energy**.

500 BCE

1800
Italian scientist Alessandro Volta creates the first **battery**.

1800

1816
Mary Shelley writes *Frankenstein*.

1837
U.S. inventor Samuel Morse invents the telegraph. It allows people to talk across long distances quickly. The telegraph is the first electric machine to make big changes in daily life.

1840

1850

1879
U.S. inventor Thomas Edison invents the first working lightbulb.

1882
Edison's Pearl Street **Power Station** brings electricity into homes and businesses.

1883
U.S. scientist Nikola Tesla invents a motor that creates **alternating current (AC)**. This allows electrical energy to travel over long-distance power lines.

1880

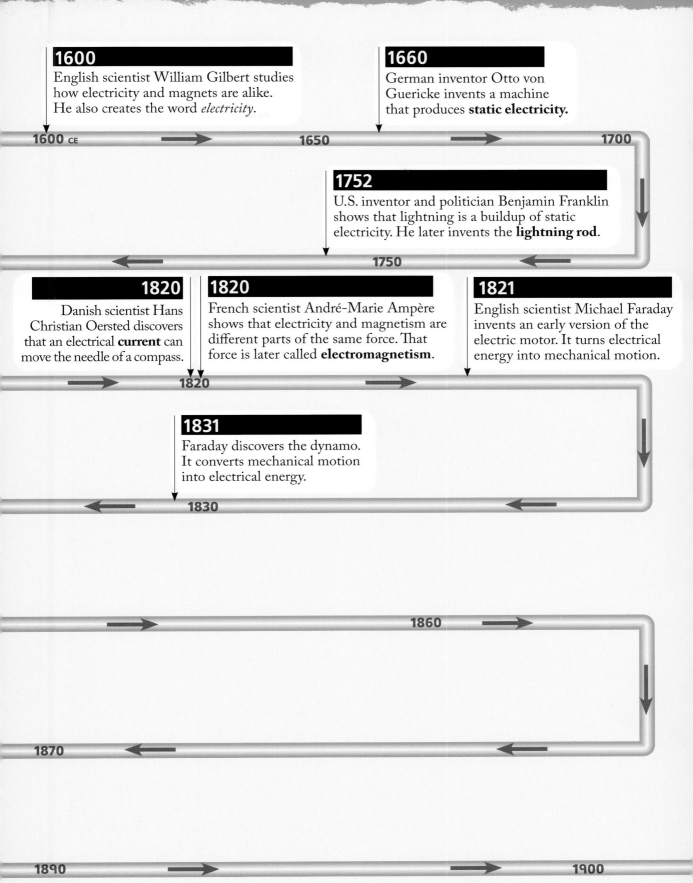

1600
English scientist William Gilbert studies how electricity and magnets are alike. He also creates the word *electricity*.

1660
German inventor Otto von Guericke invents a machine that produces **static electricity.**

1600 CE   1650   1700

1752
U.S. inventor and politician Benjamin Franklin shows that lightning is a buildup of static electricity. He later invents the **lightning rod**.

1750

1820
Danish scientist Hans Christian Oersted discovers that an electrical **current** can move the needle of a compass.

1820
French scientist André-Marie Ampère shows that electricity and magnetism are different parts of the same force. That force is later called **electromagnetism**.

1821
English scientist Michael Faraday invents an early version of the electric motor. It turns electrical energy into mechanical motion.

1820

1831
Faraday discovers the dynamo. It converts mechanical motion into electrical energy.

1830

1860

1870

1890   1900

29

Glossary

alternating current (AC) flow of electrical energy in which electric charges vibrate back and forth very quickly along wires. AC is the type of electrical energy used in homes.

atom one of the smallest units that make up substances. Splitting or combining atoms creates energy.

battery something that uses metal and chemicals to create electrical energy. Batteries use direct current, or DC.

BCE meaning "before the common era." When this appears after a date, it refers to the time before the Christian religion began.

CE meaning "common era." When this appears after a date, it refers to the time after the Christian religion began.

charge given amount of electricity. For example, rubbing a balloon on cloth builds up an electric charge.

circuit path along which an electric current moves. A current will only move if the circuit is complete and uninterrupted.

conductor material like metal that lets electric current flow easily. Most metals are popular conductors.

current flow of electrons. Electric current flows along a conductor such as a wire.

current electricity constant flow of electrons. The opposite of current electricity is static electricity.

direct current (DC) flow of electrical energy in which electrical charges flow only one way. DC is used in small devices such as flashlights.

electromagnet magnet created by using electric current. Electromagnets are the world's most powerful magnets.

electromagnetism the relationship between electricity and magnetism; also, the magnetism created by sending an electric current through a piece of metal

electron particle in an atom with a negative charge. Electrons are found in an atom's nucleus.

energy ability to cause change. Electricity is a type of energy.

generator machine that creates electrical energy. A generator provides power to your home.

insulator material that stops energy from getting through. Plastic is a popular insulator.

lightning rod invention that protects buildings from lightning. The lightning rod was invented by Benjamin Franklin.

particle object that makes up the nucleus (center) of an atom. Particles include electrons, protons, and neutrons.

pollute dirty the environment. Burning coal or oil to create electricity pollutes the air.

power station building where electricity is generated

proton particle in an atom with a positive charge. Protons are found in an atom's nucleus.

semiconductor material such as silicon that can either be an insulator or a conductor. The word is also used to mean an electronic device made of semiconducting material that is used to control electric current.

short circuit crossing of electric wires that can cause heat buildup and fire

static electricity buildup or reduction in electrons. The opposite of static electricity is current electricity.

Find Out More

Books

Landau, Elaine. *The History of Energy*. Minneapolis: Twenty-First Century Books, 2005.

Parker, Steve. *DK Eyewitness: Electricity*. New York: Dorling Kindersley, 2005.

Tagliaferro, Linda. *Thomas Edison: Inventor of the Age of Electricity*. Minneapolis: Lerner, 2003.

Walker, Sally M. *Electricity*. Minneapolis: Lerner, 2006.

Websites

Learn about electricity at this website of the U.S. Department of Energy.
www.eia.doe.gov/kids/energyfacts/sources/electricity.html

Discover electricity-related skills, such as how to read an electric meter, at this National Aeronautics and Space Administration (NASA) website. There are also some experiments, but check with a parent or teacher before trying them.
http://scifiles.larc.nasa.gov/text/kids/D_Lab/acts_electric.html

Try some safe electricity experiments at this website, but check with a parent or teacher first.
http://home.howstuffworks.com/science-projects-for-kids-current-electricity. htm

Places to visit

Museum of Science, Boston
1 Science Park
Boston, Massachusetts 02114

The museum's Theater of Electricity is home to the world's largest air-insulated Van de Graff generator, which produces dramatic displays of artificial lightning. The generator is demonstrated twice a day to help show the power of electricity.

Index